A Child's Garden of Torah

A Read-Aloud Bible

Joel Lurie Grishaver

Torah Aura Productions

Dedication

And now, therefore, write this song
for yourselves... (Deuteronomy 31.19)

For the J-Man, Joshua Parker,
whose questions and stories invited this book
and whose digitized and cyberized image
that hangs on the wall
watched over this book
like a guardian angel.

ISBN# 0-933873-14-X
3rd Printing
Copyright © 1996 Joel Lurie Grishaver
Published by Torah Aura Productions. All rights reserved.
No part of this publication may be reproduced or transmitted in any form or by any means graphic, electronic or mechanical, including photocopying, recording or by any information storage and retrieval system, without permission in writing from the publisher.

torah aura productions • 4423 Fruitland Avenue, Los Angeles, Ca 90058
(800) be-torah • (323) 585-7312 • fax (323) 585–0327 • e-mail <misrad@torahaura.com> •www.torahaura.com
manufactured in Malaysia

Foreword

Kids should have Bible dreams. They should be able to imagine themselves riding on an overcrowded ark filled with cuddly and smelly animals. They should be able to see the rainbow burst through the single window in the ark's ceiling. They should imagine themselves dancing on their first day, just after their creation in the Garden of Eden. They should have a moment of standing before an inner-mirror and trying on their parent's special gift, a coat of many colors.

Kids love the Bible, because it has it all. The Bible is not witches, dragons, space ships, ancient tombs with booby trapped giant killer boulders, and sword fights. Instead, the Bible has stories of fear and faith. The Bible knows what it is like to feel alone, to feel afraid; to be angry that someone else is loved better. It knows where your heart goes when you are the one who is left out, or the way your feelings can soar when you know that someone really loves you. It tells the story of fights after which we make up, and of the fights from which there is no making up.

The power of Bible is that it tells our story. We all have our moments of being Joseph in the limelight when it seems that we are beloved and have everything. And we all have our "in the pit time" when everything caves in and we are just trapped. We all know—in our own life story—what it is to want something that you just can't have, like Abram and Sarai craved a child. And we all have our own miracles—where God gifts us with something that we no longer believed could ever happen. Isaac is always being conceived and then birthed.

The Bible has it all—because it is our own story. A Child's Garden of Torah was written to be a first telling of these Torah stories. It was written with classroom story circles and darkened bedrooms in mind. It seeks any place where a good story can evoke a great conversation. It was designed to be a first or an early hearing and studying of these great, eternal stories. It was designed to be the beginning of a lot of dreams.

Joel Lurie Grishaver

Table of Contents

Story 1: **Creation**

Sunday:

It all started when God said,
"Let there be light."
Everything had been totally dark.
The breath of God blew across the waters.

Now there was light.
God saw that the light was GOOD!
God called the light, "Day."
God called the darkness, "Night."
Now there was evening.

Now there was morning.

This was the first day.

Monday:

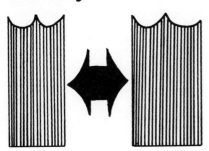

On the next day
God made nothing new.
God just said, "Let there be space."
God took the water which was everywhere
and split it in half.

All God did on Monday was put space in the middle of the water. God called this space, "Sky."

There was evening. There was morning. A second day.

Tuesday:

 On the next day
God said to the waters,
"Pull back and make room for some dryness."
The waters followed orders.
God called the waters, "Oceans."
God called the dryness, "Land."
God saw that the land and the ocean were GOOD.
God said, "Now we need plants and green growing things."
Suddenly, green things were growing everywhere.
God saw that the green things growing everywhere were GOOD.

There was evening. There was morning. A third day.

Wednesday:
On the next day
God said, "We need lights in the sky."
Suddenly, the sun, the moon, and the stars were
in their places.
The sun gave sunlight during the day.
The moon gave moonlight during the night.

The stars were there to help travelers find their way.
Wednesday was a lot like Sunday.

God saw that the new lights were GOOD.

There was evening. There was morning.
A fourth day.

Thursday:

On the next day
God started to make moving things.
God said, "Let there be birds in the sky."
God said, "Let there be fish in the seas."
And for fun, God made sea monsters, dinosaurs, and dragons.
God saw that all this new life was GOOD.
God blessed them and said,
"Live long. Have many children. Fill the earth."

Thursday was a lot like Monday.
Things were happening in the sky and in the waters.

There were birds in the sky and fish in the waters.

There was evening. There was morning. A fifth day.

Friday:

On the next day
God was ready to make the big things.
God was ready to work on land.
God said, "Let there be animals."
There were animals everywhere.
God saw that animals were GOOD.
Then God said,
"Let there be people."
Then God added:
"Let them be a little like Me."
All of a sudden there was
a woman and a man.
They were a little like God.
God made people in God's image.
God blessed them and said:
"Live long. Have many children.
Fill the earth.
And be in charge of everything."
Friday was a lot like Tuesday. Things were happening on the land.

God saw that people and everything else in the world could be VERY GOOD.

There was evening. There was morning. A sixth day.

Shabbat:

God made the world in seven days.
Six of those days God did all the work.
On *Shabbat* God rested.
God blessed Shabbat and said to Her, "You are holy."

This was the end of the beginnings.

Now the world was ready for the rest of the stories.

Hearing Questions:
What was the last day of the week of creation?
What did God create on the first day?
What was the last thing God created before Shabbat?
What did God do on Shabbat?
What did God say when God saw the things which had been created?

Imagining Questions:
God made me to be a little like God. One way I can be like God is _____.
I can be like God. One thing I can create is _____.
God said some things are good and very good.
One thing I think is good is _____.

One thing I think is very good is _____.
When I rest I like to _____.
When God rests God likes to _____.

A Torah Puzzle:
To answer these questions you may need to read parts of the story again and think hard.
How is Sunday like Wednesday?
How is Monday like Thursday?
How is Tuesday like Friday?
What was the difference between the blessing God gave animals and the blessing God gave people? How are people special?

Story 2: The Garden in Eden

God was a gardener.
God planted a garden in Eden.
The garden had lots of trees.
In the garden were lots of fruits and vegetables.

In the center of the garden God planted two special trees.

One was the Tree of Life.
One was the Tree of Knowing How to Tell Good from Evil.
God took some mud and made a body.

God blew the breath of life into the body.
It came alive and became the first human.
In Hebrew a human is called Adam.
God put Adam in the garden to take care of it.
Adam became a gardener, too.
God told Adam, "Eat all the fruits and vegetables you want."

God gave Adam one rule,
"Do not eat from the Tree of Knowing How to Tell Good from Evil.
Once you eat from it—you will begin to die."

Adam was lonely.
God made all kinds of animals.

Adam named every animal. They were interesting.
But no animal fit together with Adam.
Adam was still lonely.
Finally, God made Adam the perfect partner.
To make sure that the two of them fit together,
God took one of Adam's sides.
God built Adam's side into a woman.

Adam was now the man. His other side became the woman.
They fit together. That is the way of men and women.
They were naked. But they were not ashamed.
Adam never gave the woman a name.
They were just "Adam and his woman."

 Meanwhile,
the snake was a sneaky creature.

He talked to the woman.

He wrapped
his words around her.
He fooled her.
She ate from the
tree in the middle of the garden.
She gave Adam
some of the fruit, too.
He ate it as well.
All of a sudden things changed.

Adam and his woman saw
everything in a new way.

14

Adam and his woman knew that they were naked.
They felt ashamed.
God visited them.
They tried to hide.
God found them and made them clothes.
God told them, "Now you have to leave the garden."
God told them, "Now you have begun to die."
God told them, "Now you will have to work for your food."
And God told them, "Now women will give birth to children."

Finally, Adam gave his wife a name.
He called her, "Eve."
"Eve" means "The Life Giver."
The two of them left the garden together.

God left two angels guarding the way to Eden.

Hearing Questions:
Where was the Garden?
What was in the middle of the Garden?
What does Adam mean?
Where did Adam's partner come from?
What one rule did God give Adam and his wife?
Why did they eat the fruit?
What does Eve mean?

Imagining Questions:
What do you think the trees in the middle of the garden looked like?
How did the world look before they ate the fruit? How did it change when they ate it?
Why did the snake trick them?
What do you think is the "password" to get past the angels and back into the Garden in Eden?

Story 3: Battling Brothers: Cain and Abel

Adam and Eve had two sons.
Their names were Cain and Abel.
Abel became a shepherd.
Cain became a farmer.

One time, Cain wanted to thank God.
He scooped up some vegetables and gave them as a gift.
Abel decided to thank God, too.

He took his best sheep and gave it as a gift to God.

God said, "Yes" to Abel's gift.
God said, "No" to Cain's gift.
Cain was angry.

God talked to Cain.
God said, "You are angry."

God said, "When you do your best—it is good."
God said, "When you do a sin—it can haunt you like a ghost."

Cain didn't understand.
Cain was still angry.

Cain and Abel met in a field.
They wound up fighting.
Cain killed Abel.

God said to Cain, "Where is your brother?"
Cain answered, "I don't know.
Am I my brother's keeper?"
God said, "What have you done?
I know your brother is dead.
His blood is soaked into the ground.
The ground screamed out to me.
You have polluted the ground.
It will now be hard to farm."
God told Cain, "You need to leave."

Cain was scared.
Cain said, "People will be angry."

Cain said, "People will want to kill me."
God told Cain to go anyway.
But God protected Cain.

God gave him a sign.

Cain became a wanderer.
He went from place to place.
After a long time passed,
Cain found a wife.
Cain started his own family.

Hearing Questions:
Who were the parents in this story?
Who were the two sons?
Which son was older?
What job did Abel do? What job did Cain do?
Whose idea was it to give a gift to God?
Whose gift did God accept?
Why did Cain get scared?
What did God do for him?
How does the story end?

Imagining Questions:
How did Cain and Abel get different jobs?
Read God's words to Cain. What lesson do they teach?
Why did Cain have to leave home?
If Cain did something bad—why did God protect him?
Imagine that Cain is old and talking to his grandchildren.
Imagine that he has told them his true story. What lesson
would Cain put at the end of this story?

Story 4: The Flood

God looked at the world.
God saw a lot of people doing bad things.
God looked at people's hearts.
God thought, "People think a lot of bad thoughts."

God thought, "I must fix things."
God saw Noah. Noah was simple. Noah was good.
Noah walked the way God wants people to walk.
God said to Noah, "Make a three-floored ark."

"Fill it with two
of every kind of animal.
"Take seven
of every kosher animal.

"Put a window in the top."

Noah had a wife.
Noah had three sons.
Each son had a wife.
The eight of them came into the ark.
All the animals came into the ark.
It started to rain.

God closed the ark.
The rain came down
for 40 days and 40 nights.
The water gushed up from under ground
for 40 days and 40 nights.
The water got higher and higher for 150 days.

All the mountaintops were covered.
God remembered Noah.
God remembered Noah's wife.
God remembered Noah's three sons.
God remembered that each son had a wife.
And God remembered all the animals.
Just as on the first day of creation—
the breath of God blew across the waters.
The rain stopped falling down.

The water from under ground stopped gushing up.
The water got lower and lower for 150 days.
At last, the ark got stuck on a mountaintop.

The mountain's name was Ararat.
Noah waited 40 days. He took a raven.
He let her fly away.
The raven could find no place else to go.
Water was still everywhere.
She came back to the ark.
Then Noah took a dove. He let her fly away.

She came back to the ark. She had an olive branch in her mouth.
Noah opened the door in the ark.
Out came two of every kind of animal.
Out came seven of every Kosher animal.
Out came three sons and their wives.
Out came Noah and his wife.
The people offered gifts to God.

God liked the gifts.
God looked at the people,
just as God did at the end of the sixth day of creation.
They were a little like God,
because God had made them in God's image.
God blessed them and said,

"Live long. Have many children. Fill the earth."

For God, after the flood was like a whole new creation.
Then God looked at the people's hearts again.
God thought, "People will always think a lot of bad thoughts."
God knew, "Floods will do no good."
God said to Noah, "Let's make a covenant.

I will be with you. You will try to be good."

God made a rainbow in the clouds.
God said, "When I look at it,
I will remember my part of the covenant.

When you look at it,
you will remember your part of the covenant.

All of us will remember
that floods will do no good."
People and God started over, together, making the world better.

Hearing Questions:
When God looked at the world—what did God see?
What made Noah special?
What did God tell Noah to build?
Who was in Noah's family?
Who was in the ark?
How did Noah know the flood was over?
What did God make with Noah's family after the flood?
What are we supposed to remember when we see a rainbow?

Imagining Questions:
What did God see that made God unhappy about people?
What did God see that made God happy about Noah?
What was the hardest part of being on the ark?
Why did God pick the rainbow to be the symbol of the covenant?

Torah Puzzle:
Why is the story of the flood a lot like the story of creation?

23

Story 5: The Tower

Once all people lived in one place.
It was a valley called Shinar.
People decided to build a tower
tall enough to reach above the sky.
God decided this was not a good idea.
People build buildings out of bricks.
People build friendships out of words.

Once people decided to build a tower so tall
it would reach to the top of the sky.
Everyone worked together.
Everyone wanted the tower to succeed.
The tower was built out of bricks and out of words.

God saw the tower.

God knew that people were saying,
"We want to be as big and as tall as God.

We want to be a big and important name."
God didn't need to hear their words.
God learned it from their bricks.
God knew that talking can be good.
Talking can make a friend happy.
But, words can do bad things, too.
God made a plan.

God saw to it that the bricks did not reach above the sky.
The bricks wound up in a sloppy pile.

25

God babbled the way people spoke.
God confused their words.

Their sounds were now as messy as their piles of bricks.

Today we call the place where the tower used to be the Land of Babel.
People gave up and moved away.
The next day they had to learn how to talk all over.
This time they wanted to learn how to make their words reach
above the sky.

Hearing Questions:
Where did people live?
Who lived there?
What did they decide?
What did God decide?
What happened?

Imagining Questions:
How can bricks be a good thing?
How can bricks be a bad thing?
How can words be a good thing?
How can words be a bad thing?
What would have been a good thing for the people in the Valley of Shinar to build?
What is one thing you can do to help your words get higher than the sky?

Story 6: Abram, Sarai & Family

Adam had a son who had a son. This son had a son. So it went.
Ten sons from Adam was Noah.
Noah had a son who had a son. This son had a son. So it went.

Ten sons from Noah was Abram.

Abram, Sarai, Lot, and Tera<u>h</u> lived in a city called Ur.
Tera<u>h</u> was the father.
Abram was the son.
Sarai was his wife.
Lot was Abram's nephew.

They all wanted to go to a land called Canaan.
On the way they stopped in Haran.

Terah died there.
God spoke to Abram and told him, "Go to the Land I will show you."

God led him to Canaan.

God spoke to Abram.
God promised him many things.
God promised that Abram and Sarai
would be the parents of a new nation.
God promised to bless them and their family.
God led them to the Land of Canaan.

Soon, the Land of Canaan will get a new name.

Soon Abram's family will get a new name, too.
The family and the land will share a name.
They will both be called Israel.
Coming to Israel was the start of something good.
Abram and Sarai were the first Jews.
Abram and Sarai were the start of something good, too.

Hearing Questions:
What was the name of the son in this story?
What was the name of the wife in this story?
What was the name of the father in this story?
Who else is part of the family?
Where did the family want to go?
Where was the family at the end of the story?

Imagining Questions:
Later on, Abram and Sarai became the first Jews. Why do you think God picked them?
What was the best thing that they found in the Land of Canaan?
What do you think Abram and Sarai dreamed about?

Story 7: **Sarah Laughs**

A long time ago God made a promise.
God told Abram and Sarai:
"Your family will grow into a great nation."
Abram and Sarai are now old.
They have no children.
A family without children
cannot grow into a great nation.

Abram and Sarai are sad.

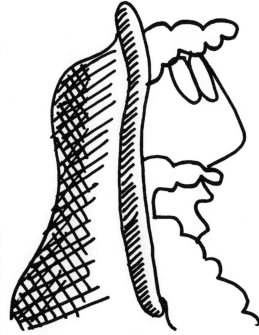

God gave Abram a new name: "Abraham."
God gave Sarai a new name: "Sarah."
God told Abraham, "Look at the stars.
Count them.
As many people will grow from Sarah and Abraham
as there are stars in the sky."

God told Abraham,
"Pick up a handful of sand.
Count the grains.
As many people will grow from Sarah and Abraham

as there are grains of sand in the world."
One hot day Abraham was sitting in the door of his tent.
Three strangers came walking along.
Abraham got up and RAN to them and asked them to
PLEASE be his guests.
The strangers said, "Yes."
Everyone in the camp HURRIED to take care
of them.
Abraham washed their feet.
Sarah baked bread.
A servant roasted a lamb.

Abraham and Sarah made their guests welcome.
They RAN and HURRIED
and tried to PLEASE them.

They fed them dinner.
After dinner one stranger said,
"Sarah will have a son."
Sarah was old and wrinkled.
Sarah knew that she was too old to have children.
She heard the stranger's words and laughed.
God then spoke and told them that this promise would come true.
Soon they had a son.
They gave him a name which means "laughter."

They called him Isaac.
That night Abraham looked at the stars differently.

Hearing Questions:
What did God promise Abram and Sarai?
Why were they sad?
What was Abram's new name?
What was Sarai's new name?
Where did God tell Abraham to look?
When three visitors came, what did Sarah and Abraham do?
What did the visitors tell them?
What did Sarah do next?

What did God do next?
What did Sarah and Abraham name their son?
What does Isaac mean?

Imagining Questions:
What kind of person do you think Isaac became?
How did having the name "laughter" change him?
What do you think Abraham and Sarah saw when they looked at the stars?

Story 8: Sodom Goes Boom

Abraham had a nephew named Lot.

Lot came to Canaan with Sarah and Abraham.

For a while they all lived together.

After a while they all got rich.

They all had many camels, many sheep, many cattle and many tents.

After a while trouble started.

After a while they were too many to live in one place.

Lot's shepherds began to fight
with Abraham's shepherds.

It looked like big trouble.
But Abraham was smart. He told Lot,
"*Sh'lom Bayit*, family peace, is most important."
He said, "If you go north, I will go south.
If you go south, I will go north."
Lot picked the plains near the city of Sodom.
Abraham went the other way.

All of this happened long before Isaac was born.

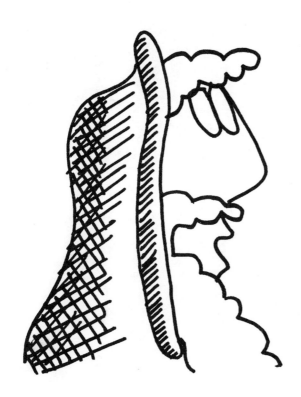

The three visitors who came to Abraham and Sarah were really angels.
They told them about Isaac
and then left.
Two of them went on to Sodom.

They went to see Lot
and his family.
That day God and Abraham
had a meeting.
They talked about
the city of Sodom.
God said, "I want to destroy it
because the people are evil."

Abraham said to God,
"Will not the Judge of the earth act justly?"

Abraham told God, "It would be unfair to
punish the good people along with the evil ones."

Abraham and God made a deal about Sodom.
They agreed that if there were ten good people in the city

God would not destroy it.

God needed to do homework.
God needed to check out the city.
The two angels were sent to visit it.

Lot was Abraham's nephew.
He did just as Abraham had done.
He made the strangers welcome.
He invited them into his home.

But, things were not good.
Lot and his family
were the only good people in the city
(and there were not 10 of them).
All of the people of Sodom were wicked.
The people of Sodom came to Lot.
They asked Lot to give them the strangers.
The people wanted to hurt them—just for fun.

Lot said, "No."

The angels told Lot to get his family out of town.
Lot and his family left.
The angels had told them not to look back.
Everyone in Lot's family listened to these orders except for Lot's wife.
Sodom was destroyed.
Lot's wife was turned into a pillar of salt.

Hearing Questions:
Who was Lot?
Why did Abraham and Lot separate?
Where did Lot go?
How did God feel about Sodom? What did God want to do?
What did Abraham say about God's plan?
What deal did they make?
Who went to Sodom?
Who was just like Abraham and welcomed the visitors?
What happened next?
How does the story end?

Imagining Questions:
Why did God tell Abraham about the plans for Sodom?
What did God see the people of Sodom doing that got God angry?
Why do you think Lot's wife looked back?

Story 9: Rebekkah Really Cares

This is a story with ten camels.
It is a story about finding a wife for Isaac.
In this story the camels pick the right woman.

Rebekkah becomes Isaac's wife by being nice to camels.
Abraham was really old.
His wife Sarah was dead.
His son Isaac had no wife.
Abraham sent his servant on a secret mission.
The secret mission was to find
the right woman to be Isaac's wife.
His secret weapon was ten camels.

The servant went back to Ur.
Ur was Abraham's original home.
The servant and the camels went to the well.
He had a secret plan.
He and the camels sat there.
The servant asked women
to pour a little water for him from their jars.
The question was a secret test.
To be the winner
you had to say more than just "Yes."
One woman
said more than just "Yes."
It turned out
she was from the same family as Abraham.

41

Her name was Rebekkah.

Rebekkah brought water for the servant.
Then she did more.
She did something he didn't ask for.
She saw something which needed doing.
She won the prize.
She became Mrs. Isaac because—
she saw and understood and then did.

She said, "And I will bring all the water
your camels need."

The servant saw that she was just like Abraham.
She, too, RAN and HURRIED and tried to PLEASE strangers.
She became the perfect wife for Isaac.

They fell in love the moment they met.

The camel plan worked.

Hearing Questions:
In this story, what did Abraham want to find?
Who did he send to do the finding?
What did the servant take?
Where did the servant go?
What did the servant do?
What was the secret plan?
Who passed the test?
How did the story end?

Imagining Questions:
Why did the servant want to test the women?
What made Rebekkah the perfect wife for Isaac?
Isaac and Rebekkah looked at each other and fell in love.
What do you think they each saw?
What do you think they did on their first date?

Story 10: Battling Brothers: Jacob & Esau

Isaac and Rebekkah had twin sons.
Before they were born,
they fought to see who would be born first.

Esau won and became the oldest.
Esau was the oldest brother.
His name means "Hairy."
He was big and tough.
He was a hunter.

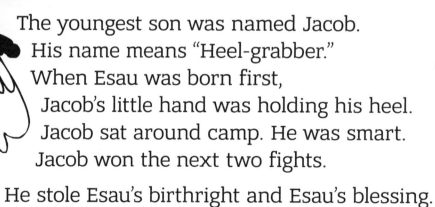

The youngest son was named Jacob.
His name means "Heel-grabber."
When Esau was born first,
Jacob's little hand was holding his heel.
Jacob sat around camp. He was smart.
Jacob won the next two fights.

He stole Esau's birthright and Esau's blessing.

Isaac was the father in this story.

He was old.

He couldn't see well.

His favorite son was Esau.

Jacob liked to eat meat.

Esau hunted and brought him meat.

The mother in this story was Rebekkah.

Her favorite son was Jacob.

She helped him a lot.

First, Jacob stole Esau's birthright.
This is the "right" to own all of your father's stuff after your father dies.
In those days the birthright always went to the oldest son.
But one day Esau was hungry.
He was so hungry that he thought he was going to die.
Jacob was making bean soup.
Esau said, "Give me some soup."
Jacob said,
"Give me your birthright."
They made a deal.
Esau gave Jacob all of Isaac's stuff
for a bowl of bean soup.

Second, Jacob stole
Esau's blessing.
Rebekkah
helped him.

One day Isaac sent Esau to hunt for meat.
Isaac promised to bless Esau that day.
Rebekkah had a plan.
She made Jacob do it.
She dressed him up in Esau's clothes.
She made him wear fur to make him feel "hairy."
She sent him with meat to feed Isaac.
Almost blind Isaac was tricked.
He said these holy words to the wrong son:
"May God give you the dew of heaven and the fat of the earth."

It is also possible that Isaac tricked them.
Maybe he wanted them all to think he didn't know.
We'll never know for sure.

Hearing Questions:
Who were the parents in this story?
Who were the twin sons?
What does "Esau" mean?
What does "Jacob" mean?
What two things did Jacob take from Esau?
Who helped him get the blessing?

Imagining Questions:
Why do you think Esau sold his birthright?
Why do you think Rebekkah liked Jacob better?
Do you think Jacob fooled Isaac or do you think Isaac fooled Jacob?

Story 11: **Jacob's Dream**

Jacob left home for two reasons.
REASON ONE: He wanted to find a wife.
REASON TWO: He was afraid that his brother Esau would kill him.

Jacob walked all day.
He made camp for the night.
He made a pillow out of a stone.
That night he had a dream about a ladder.
Its feet were on the earth. Its top reached to heaven.

In the dream Jacob saw angels moving in two directions.
He saw angels going up.
He saw angels going down.

Jacob woke up in the morning.
He knew the dream was a sign from God.
He said, "God is in this place."
He took the stone pillow and made it into a marker.
He poured oil on it.

He said, "This place is God's house."
He called it "Bet El."
Bet El means God's House.
Jacob said,
"God was in this place
and I did not know it."
That happens to all of us
sometimes—
we can be close to God
and not even know it.

Hearing Questions:
Why did Jacob leave home?
What did Jacob use for a pillow?
What did Jacob dream?
What did Jacob know about the dream?
What did he do in the morning?

Imagining Questions:
What lesson did God try to teach Jacob through the dream?
How can we be close to God and not even know it?

Story 12: Israel's Family

Some people say, "What goes around—comes around."
It means that what you do to someone—
someone else will probably do to you.
This is a story about "What goes around—comes around."

Jacob had tricked Esau two times.
Jacob stole the birthright.
Jacob stole the blessing.
Jacob came to Paddan Aram to hide from Esau.
Jacob came to Paddan Aram to find a wife.
He fell in love with Rachel. She had a sister Leah.
Rachel and Leah were a lot like Jacob and Esau.
Laban was the father of both girls.

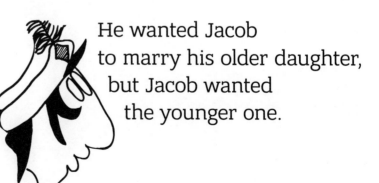

He wanted Jacob
to marry his older daughter,
but Jacob wanted
the younger one.

At the wedding Laban tricked Jacob and switched daughters.
Jacob thought he was marrying Rachel.
The bride covered her face.
After the wedding Jacob learned that his bride was Leah, not Rachel.
He had been tricked.
Jacob married first Leah and then Rachel.
He became the father of thirteen children.

Leah and Rachel were a lot like Jacob and Esau.
They each wanted to be first.
They had a contest.

They each wanted to be the mother of the most children.
They used all kinds of tricks to have the most.
In the end, Jacob and his wives had thirteen children.
The twelve sons' names were Reuben, Simeon, Levi, Judah, Issachar,
Zebulun, Benjamin, Dan, Naphtali, Gad, Asher, and Joseph.
The one daughter was named Dinah.

Before Jacob came to Paddan Aram
he made a deal with God.
He said, "If God stays with me,
if God protects me,
if God gives me food to eat
and clothing to wear,
if I return safely to my father's house—
then I will make God my God
and give God gifts."

Some people say, "What goes around—comes around."
In this story Jacob, who played tricks, got tricked.
In this story Jacob, who made a promise to God, kept that promise.

Hearing Questions:
Why did Jacob come to Paddan Aram?
Whom did he meet?
Whom did he marry first?
Whom did he marry second?
What happened to his family?
What did Jacob promise God?

Imagining Questions:
How were Leah and Rachel like Jacob and Esau?
What "went around" and what "came around" in this story?

Story 13: The Wrestling Match

Jacob was coming home.
He was scared.

He was afraid of Esau.
Isaac had two sons, Jacob and Esau.
Jacob stole the birthright
and then the blessing from Esau.
Then he went away.
Jacob was with Laban
for 20 years.
He had two wives,
Leah and Rachel.

He now had twelve children.
Number thirteen was on the way.
Isaac, his father, had died while he was away.
Jacob was coming home.

He was scared that his brother Esau would still be mad.
He was scared that Esau would fight with him.

Jacob came back to Canaan.

On his first day back in Canaan he saw angels.
He knew God was still with him.
Jacob had seen angels on his last night in Canaan, too.

It was his first night back in Canaan.
Jacob made a camp.
In the morning he would see Esau again.
He sent away his family to keep them safe.

That night he was alone.
That night he wrestled with a stranger.
They wrestled all night. No one could win.
That night Jacob got a new name.

The night was ending.
The stranger said, "I must go."
Jacob said, "Give me a blessing and I will let you go."
The angel gave Jacob a new name: "Israel."
He said, "Israel means
One who can wrestle with God."

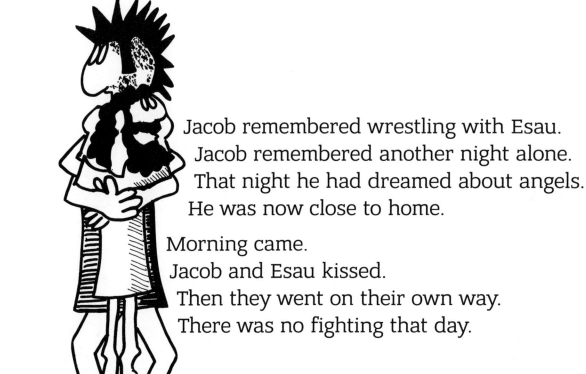

Jacob remembered wrestling with Esau.
Jacob remembered another night alone.
That night he had dreamed about angels.
He was now close to home.

Morning came.
Jacob and Esau kissed.
Then they went on their own way.
There was no fighting that day.

Hearing Questions:
Who was Jacob's brother?
Why was Jacob afraid?
What did Jacob see when he got to Canaan?
What did Jacob do with his family?
What happened when Jacob was alone?
How did the stranger bless him?
What does "Israel" mean?
What happened when Jacob and Esau met?

Imagining Questions:
Who did Jacob wrestle?
Why didn't Jacob and Esau fight this time?
How do you think becoming Israel changed Jacob's life?

Story 14: Joseph: The Favorite

Jacob had a big family.
Many wives.
Many servants. Many kids.

Just like his mother
and father,
Jacob had a favorite son.
Joseph was his favorite son.

Jacob loved Joseph more than his other children.

Jacob gave Joseph a special gift.
Jacob gave Joseph a coat of many colors.

Joseph had dreams
that said he was the best son.
Joseph's first dream was about grain.

This was the dream.
Everyone in the family made a bundle of grain.
Then all of the bundles bowed down to Joseph's bundle.

Joseph had a second dream.
It was also about bowing down.
In this dream the sun, moon and
stars bowed down to Joseph.

The other brothers hated his coat.
They hated his dreams.
They hated him.
They threw him in a pit.
They poured blood on his coat.
They told Jacob he was dead.
They sold him to be a slave in Egypt.

Hearing Questions:
Who was Jacob's favorite son?
What did Jacob give Joseph?
What two things did Joseph dream?
What did Joseph's brothers do?
What happened to Joseph's coat?

Imagining Questions:
Why didn't Jacob stop the trouble between his sons?
What do you think Joseph's dreams meant?
What do you think Joseph's coat looked like?

Story 15: Joseph Goes to Jail and Then Works for Pharaoh

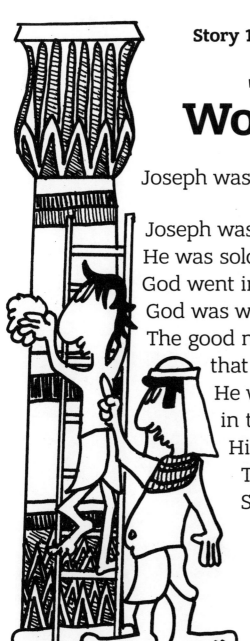

Joseph was *lucky* and **unlucky**.

Joseph was brought to Egypt.
He was sold as a slave.
God went into slavery with Joseph.
God was with him.
The good news was
        that his master liked Joseph a lot.
        He was made the number one slave
        in the house.
        His master's name was Potiphar.
        The bad news was Potiphar's wife.
        She got mad at Joseph.

She lied about him.
She had him thrown in jail.

Being thrown in jail is like
being thrown in a pit.
It was bad being in jail.
God went to jail
with Joseph.
God was with him.
But even in jail
there was good news.

The jailer liked Joseph
and helped him.
Just like Potiphar,
the jailer made Joseph
his number one helper.

Two people in jail had dreams.
They were Pharaoh's butler
and Pharaoh's baker.
Once again we have two dreams.

These two people used to work for Pharaoh
but each had made him angry.
Joseph was good at dreams.
They told him their dreams.

Pharaoh's butler had a dream
about carrying Pharaoh's cup.

Pharaoh's baker had a dream
about carrying Pharaoh's bread.

Joseph told each what their dreams meant.
For the baker it was bad news.
For the butler it was good news.
For Joseph it became very good news.

Once again we have two dreams.
This time Pharaoh had two dreams.
In one dream
seven skinny cows ate seven fat cows.
In one dream seven skinny ears of corn
ate seven fat ears of corn.
No one knew what they meant.
But, the butler remembered Joseph.

Joseph was brought
to Pharaoh.

Again God went with him.
Joseph said,
"Your two dreams are messages from God.
Egypt will have seven fat years of good crops.
Next will come seven hungry years.
You must plan to keep the hungry years
from eating up everything and everyone."
Just like Potiphar, just like the jailer—
Pharaoh put Joseph in charge.

Joseph was *lucky* that his father loved him
but *unlucky* that his brothers hated him.
He was *unlucky* to become a slave
but *lucky* that his master liked him.
Joseph was *lucky* to become the head slave
but *unlucky* that his master's wife
lied about his doing wrong.
He was *unlucky* to be thrown in jail,
but *lucky* to become the jailer's favorite.
Joseph was *lucky*
that two of Pharaoh's servants went to jail.
Joseph was *luckier* that they told him their dreams—
and that he knew what they meant.
But—Jacob was *most lucky*
that God was with him always.

Hearing Questions:
How did Jacob get to Egypt?
What job did he get in Egypt?
What good thing happened in Potiphar's house?
What bad thing happened in Potiphar's house?
What happened to Joseph in jail?
Who in jail had dreams?
Who in Egypt had dreams?
What did Pharaoh's two dreams mean?

Imagining Questions:
Why does everyone have two dreams?
Why was Joseph so lucky?

Story 16: And Finally—Jacob Comes to Egypt

Remember?
Pharaoh had two dreams and Joseph told him what they meant.
They meant seven good years followed by seven bad years.
Pharaoh put Joseph in charge of food.
During the seven good years Egypt saved and saved food.

When the hunger came they had food.
Egypt had lots of food.
People came from everywhere
to buy food in Egypt.

Jacob sent most of his sons to Egypt to get food
because there was none left in Canaan.
He kept Benjamin at home.
Benjamin was the youngest son.
Benjamin was Jacob's new favorite.

Ten brothers came to Egypt and
bowed in front of the Egyptian food boss.
They did not know that it was Joseph.
His dreams came true.

Joseph tested them.
He made them go back to Canaan and get Benjamin.
They brought Benjamin.
Then he tricked them and made it look like Benjamin was a thief.
He said he would keep Benjamin as a slave.
These brothers had sold him as a slave.
He wanted to know if they had changed.
Judah was an older brother.
He said, "Keep me and let him go."

Joseph began to cry.
He said, "I am Joseph your brother."

Everybody forgave everybody.
The family made up.
Everyone moved down to Egypt.

Joseph said, "God was always with me.
God sent me to Egypt to save lives."
Everyone cried. It was a good crying.

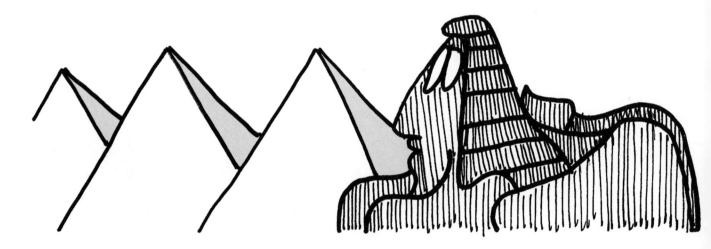

Hearing Questions:
What did Egypt do for seven years?
Why did the brothers come down to Egypt?
Who did not come?
How did Joseph test his brothers?
How did they pass the test?
How does the story end?

Imagining Questions:
How was Benjamin like Joseph?
Why did Joseph test his brothers?
Did Joseph's dreams all come true?

Story 17: Baby Moses

Years went by.
Seventy people came to Egypt with Jacob.
In the beginning his whole family was only seventy people big.
It was a big family, but not a nation.
Do you remember that God promised Abraham and Sarah two things?
God promised that the Families-of-Israel would become a nation.
God promised that the Families-of-Israel would own the Land of Israel.

Years passed.
One promise came true.
The Families-of-Israel were still in Egypt,
and they had grown into a nation of thousands and thousands.

Egypt got a new Pharaoh.
The old Pharaoh was Joseph's friend.
The new Pharaoh was not Joseph's friend.
The new Pharaoh was scared of the Families-of-Israel.
The new Pharaoh acted like he hated
the Families-of-Israel.
He was mean to them.
He turned them into slaves.
He wanted to hurt them.
He made them work hard.
He made their life bitter.

Just as Joseph was once a slave in Egypt,
now his whole family became slaves in Egypt.
Just as Joseph was freed from slavery,
his whole family hoped that they would go free, too.
Just as one of God's promises came true,
they hoped that the other promise would come true, too.

Pharaoh did many mean things.

This was the meanest.

Pharaoh ordered all baby Israelite boys to be thrown into the Nile River.

The babies could not swim.

They all died.

One Jewish family followed Pharaoh's orders in a funny way.

This is their story.

When their new son was born

the mother looked at the boy and saw that he was GOOD.

This mother looked at her son in the same way

God looked at the seven days of creation.

Both of them looked and saw that their creations were GOOD.

This family followed Pharaoh's orders.

They threw their son in the Nile River.

This family also added their own twist.

They put their son in a basket.

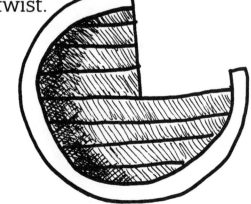

The basket was covered with
pitch—just like Noah's ark.

The basket floated just like Noah's ark.

The baby was kept safe from the waters.

Just as creation was the start of GOOD things,
this boy would be the start of wonderful new things.
Just as Noah's ark was a way of saving life,
this boy would change thousands and thousands of lives.

An Egyptain woman found the boy in the basket
and took him.
She decided to make him her son.
This woman was Pharaoh's daughter.
She gave her new son the name "Moses."
Moses means, "I took him out of the water."
Sometimes God likes little twists in life.
A Jewish boy became a prince of Egypt.

Miriam was hiding in the bushes.
She was Moses' sister.
When Pharaoh's daughter took the child
Miriam came running.

Miriam had been hiding and watching.
She told Pharaoh's daughter
that she knew a good nurse.
The nurse could take care of the baby.
Pharaoh's daughter asked to meet the nurse.
This was another little twist.
The nurse was Yoheved.
She was Moses' real mother.
She helped to raise her son.
A Prince of Egypt was raised by a Jewish woman.
Yoheved gave Moses away and still raised him.

Moses grew up.
One day Moses saw an Egyptian boss hitting a Jewish slave.
He got mad.
He killed the Egyptian.
This was another twist.

A Prince of Egypt
became an outlaw for helping a Jew.
Moses then had to run away from Egypt.

We are still waiting for God's second promise to come true.

Hearing Questions:
Who is the bad guy in this story?
What did Pharaoh do to the Jews?
What was the worst thing Pharaoh ordered?
What did one family do?
What happened to their baby?
What name did Pharaoh's daughter give the baby?
Who raised Moses?
What happened when Moses grew up?

Imagining Questions:
Why was Pharaoh mean to the Jewish people?
What "twists" happened in this story?
Do you think Moses felt more like a Jew or more like an Egyptian?
Why does it take such a long time for God's promises to come true?

Torah Puzzle:
The Torah makes the story of Moses' birth sound like the story of creation. What do the two things have in common?
The Torah makes the story of Moses' basket sound like the story of Noah's ark. What do the two things have in common?

Story 18: The Burning Bush

Moses ran away from Egypt.
He came to the Land of Midian.
He married Jethro's daughter.
Her name was Tziporah.
Her father Jethro was the High Priest of Midian.

Moses was no longer a prince.
Now he had a new job.
Moses worked as a shepherd.

One day he led his sheep far into
the wilderness.
They went to a far away place.
They went to a place Moses would
visit again.
They came close to Mt. Sinai.
This day would be a lot like
another day at Mt. Sinai.

Moses saw a burning bush.
The bush burned
and burned.
The fire
did not eat it up.
The bush kept
burning and burning.
God spoke to Moses
from the bush.
God told him
to go back to Egypt.

God said,
"Go back to Egypt.
Tell My people
I remember them.
I will make
them free.
I will be their God."

Moses said, "They will not believe me."
God said, "Take your staff.
Throw it on the ground."
Moses did what God said.
A miracle happened.
The staff became a snake.
God said, "Do this and they will believe you."

God said, "I will make you My people.
I will give you the Land of Israel."

These were the same promises that God promised Sarah and Abraham.
God remembered.
Moses went back to Egypt.
He took his brother, Aaron.

This was the beginning of the Exodus.
Soon, the Families-of-Israel would all meet God at Mt. Sinai.
The promise of Israel was beginning to come true.

Hearing Questions:
Where did Moses go?
Who did he meet there?
What was his new job?
Where did he take his sheep?
What did God tell him?
What happened at the end of the story?

Imagining Questions:
Why did God pick a bush for a place to talk to Moses?
Why was Moses afraid to follow God's command?
What will happen at Mount Sinai in the future? How will it be like this story?

Story 19: Blood, Frogs, Lice, Wild Animals, Sick Cows, Boils, Hail, Locusts, Darkness, & a Visit From the Angel of Death

Plague 1:
It started with blood.
God made all the water
turn into blood.
Aaron took Moses' staff and held
it over the Nile.
The Nile turned to blood.

Pharaoh didn't change his mind.
He still said "No" to Israel.
His heart was hard.

Plague 2:

Next came the frogs.
Frogs were everywhere.
Aaron went to the Nile again.
He took Moses' staff
and held it over the water.
This time out of the water
came lots and lots of frogs.
Pharaoh didn't change his mind.
He still said "No" to Israel.
His heart was hard.

After that, all kinds of bad things started to happen.
Moses told Pharaoh that God wanted
to take Israel out of Egypt.
Pharaoh said "No" nine times.
His heart was hard every time.

Plague 3 was lice in everyone's hair.
Pharaoh said, "No."

Plague 4 was wild animals.
Pharaoh said, "No."

Plague 5 was all the cows getting sick.
Pharaoh said, "No."

Plague 6 was boils on everyone's skin.
Pharaoh said, "No."

Plague 7 was big hailstones
falling and breaking everything.
Pharaoh said, "No."

Plague 8 was locusts
eating all of the food.
Pharaoh said, "No."

Plague 9 was
the next to last.
Pharaoh said, "No."
Moses held his arm
to the sky.
Everything went
black.
The ninth plague
was darkness.

Plague 10:

Pharaoh didn't change his mind.
He still said "No" to Israel.
His heart was still hard.
Then God made the last plague.
This was the hardest and strictest
plague.
It was also the saddest.
This plague brought many tears.
The tenth plague was the death of
every oldest Egyptian son.
This time Pharaoh said, "Yes."

Now the Families-of-Israel
could bake their matzah and leave Egypt in a hurry.

Now they were on their way to the Promised Land.

Hearing Questions:
What do we call the bad things that God made happen to
the Egyptians?
How many were there?
The first plague was blood. What happened?
The second plague was frogs. What happened?
Why didn't Pharaoh let the Jewish people go?
What was the last plague?
What happened this time?

Imagining Questions:
God used power to do plagues. Why didn't God just use
power to take the Families-of-Israel out of Egypt?
What is it like to have a hard heart?
What was the next to worst plague?
What does it feel like to see a miracle?

Story 20: Miriam's Song

"Hurry!" Everyone was shouting "Hurry!" or "Run!"
It was hurry to pack.
It was hurry out of Egypt.
Everyone knew that Pharaoh might change his mind again.

The women were in a big rush.
They started to make bread.
They mixed flour and water.

They ran
out of time.
They had to run.
Their bread had
no time to rise.
It came out
as matzah.

They packed
their matzah
and ran.

God told the Families-of-Israel in Egypt to talk to their neighbors.
They were given gold and jewels.
The Families-of-Israel took these things with them.
They kept them.
The gold and jewels were payment for
400 years of working as slaves.

The women also packed
musical instruments.
These would be very important
later on.
They would use them very soon.
All the women took tambourines.

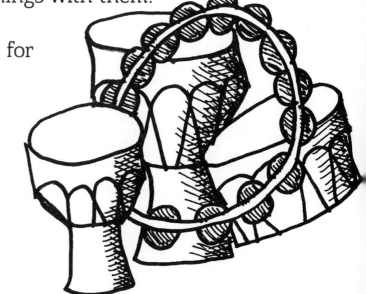

The Families-of-Israel ran all the way to the Reed Sea.
No one could swim.
The Families-of-Israel stopped.
There was nowhere to go.
They were right to hurry.
Pharaoh did change his mind.
He ran after them.
Pharaoh and the Egyptian army were right behind them.
There was nowhere to go.

The Families-of-Israel were scared.
God made a miracle.
God divided the sea so they could escape.
The Reed Sea divided.
The Families-of-Israel crossed the sea safely.
Pharaoh and his army didn't.
Then the sea closed.
The Egyptians were caught in the middle.

Miriam took out her tambourine
and began to sing and dance.
All the women joined her.
Now was the time
they needed the tambourines.
God had to be thanked.
The women thanked God
 in song and dance.

The men sang and danced, too.

Hearing Questions:
What were the last things Israel did in Egypt?
Where did they run to?
Why were they in a hurry?
What did God do?
What happened to the Egyptians?
What did the women do with the tambourines?

Imagining Questions:
Why were the tambourines needed?
How did the women know that they would be needed?
Was it right to steal the Egyptians' jewels?
Did God like their singing and dancing?

Story 21: The Ten Commandments

Moses took his sheep to Mt. Sinai.
There he met God.
Now, Moses led the Families-of-Israel
to Mt. Sinai.
Here they would all meet God.
They made camp. They got ready.

The mountain smoked.
There was thunder and lightning.

God spoke to all of Israel.
God taught Torah to the people.
When God created the world, God used words.
God said only ten things
to make everything.
God was creating
something new at Mt. Sinai.
God again said ten things.
God spoke.
The people all said, "We will do. We will listen."

Moses went up the mountain to get it in writing.

God said, "I am Adonai your God."
Every Jew heard these words.

God went on teaching. "No idols.
No lies using God's name.
Remember Shabbat.
Honor parents.
No murder.
No cheating on your family.
No stealing.
No lying.
No wanting
something that
belongs to
someone else."

The people all said, "We will do. We will listen."
Moses went up Mt. Sinai.
He spent 40 days and 40 nights studying Torah with God.
There was a lot more to learn than just ten things.
Those ten things were only the beginning.
Moses started down the mountain.
In his hands were two tablets of stone.

Even 40 days and 40 nights was just the beginning
of learning and living Torah.
We are still working on it. That is part of our promise.
"We will do. We will listen."
Reading this book is part of the listening and part of the doing.

Hearing Questions:
Where did this story happen?
When had Moses been here before?
What happened on that trip to Mount Sinai?
How many things did God say to the Families-of-Israel?
What did Moses do next?
How long did he spend?

Imagining Questions:
What does "We will do. We will listen." mean?
Why does it take so long to learn Torah?
How was being at Mt. Sinai like being at the creation of
the world?

Story 22: The Golden Calf

Moses spent a long time on Mt. Sinai.
He was up on Mount Sinai
studying Torah with God.
Learning Torah takes a long time.
40 days and 40 nights is a long time.
Everyone else was scared.
They thought Moses was not coming back.
The people got scared
and asked for a new god.
Aaron was Moses' brother.
He made an idol for them.

Moses was writing down the
Ten Commandments.

One of them was "No idols."

Aaron took the people's gold
earrings and melted them.
He made a golden calf.
It was to be a new god.

The Ten Commandments say, "No idols."

Moses came down the mountain.
He was carrying two tablets with the Ten Commandments.
He saw the calf.
He almost fainted.
He dropped the tablets.
They broke.

He took the calf and smashed it.
He ground it into a fine powder.
He mixed it with water.
He made everyone who had helped with the calf drink it.

This was a day that God was not very happy with the Families-of-Israel.
Moses was not very happy, either.
He had to go up Mt. Sinai and do everything over again.

Still, when the Families-of-Israel said, "We are sorry,"
God forgave them.
Moses forgave them, too.
Moses went back up Mt. Sinai to start over again.

Even broken commandments can usually be fixed.

Hearing Questions:
Where does this story take place?
Where was Moses?
Who was in the camp?
How long was Moses gone?
What happens?
When Moses saw the calf what happened?
How does this story end?

Imagining Questions:
Why did the people give up on God and Moses?
Why did they think that a golden calf could be a god?
Why did Moses make them drink the calf?
Why did God forgive them?

Story 23: God Lives in the Middle of the Families-of-Israel

The golden calf was a bad thing.
The people had missed God and Moses.
When they were gone people got in trouble.
God learned one thing.
There must always be a place
where people could get close to God.
God made plans for a place
where God would always be a neighbor.
It was called the *Mishkan*.
It could be moved from place to place.
Mishkan comes from a word
that means "neighborhood."
No matter where Israel moved,
God was their neighbor.
God gave the plans to Moses.
Moses picked Betzalel to build it.

Here are some things that Betzalel made:

The Ark of the Covenant was a golden box.
In it were the Ten Commandments and the Torah.
There were two winged cherubim on top.
They were looking face-to-face at each other.
They looked like best friends.
They also looked like the angels who guarded the way to the Garden in Eden.

The Ark was kept in the inside room.
This is the place where God was found.
It was called the Holy of Holies.
People have an inside place, too, which is their own Holy of Holies.

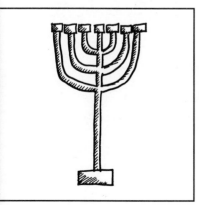

The Menorah was a lamp
with places for seven flames.
One flame was for each day of creation.

The Ner Tamid was a fire that never went out.
It was kept in the altar.
It was like the fire on top of Mt. Sinai.
It was like the burning bush.
It showed that God was always near.

Betzalel was the artist
who made the *Mishkan*.
The *Mishkan* is the place
where God is always our neighbor.

Hearing Questions:

What did God learn from the golden calf?

What was the name of the place God wanted the Families-of-Israel to build?

What does *Mishkan* mean?

Where were the Ten Commandments kept?

Where was the Ark of the Covenant kept?

What had seven flames?

What kept burning forever?

Imagining Questions:

Why was the Torah guarded by the same angels who watched the way to Eden?

Where is your Holy of Holies?

Why do we need to remember the seven days of creation every week?

Where can you go to remember that God's light never goes out?

Moses Hits the Rock

Everyone makes mistakes.
This is a sad story.
It is a story about being angry.
Miriam had died.
She was Moses' sister.
She was an important leader, too.

The people were sad.
They were hungry.

They
wanted
water.

They screamed, "Give us water! Give us food!"
God was ready to make a miracle.
God was going to make water come from a rock.

God told Moses to talk to the rock
and ask for water.

The Families-of-Israel yelled at Moses.
The Families-of-Israel
screamed at Moses.
They said, "Give us food.
Give us water."

Moses got mad.
He lost his temper.
He took his staff
and hit the rock.

He was mad at the people and hit the rock.
The rock gave off water.
The Families-of-Israel had plenty to drink.
Moses lost his future.
God said, "Because you did this, you cannot go into Israel."

This gave Joshua a big chance.
Joshua would be
the new Jewish leader.

Aaron ran the *Mishkan*.
He was the head *Kohein*,
or priest.
He died.
His son took over
and became the head *Kohein*.

Joshua's time was coming, too.

Hearing Questions:
Who was Miriam?
What did the people want?
What did God plan?
What did Moses do?
What was Moses' punishment?
Who was Aaron?
What happened when he died?

Imagining Questions:
How did Miriam's death make the people feel?
Why did Moses get so angry?
Was "You can't go into Israel" the right punishment for Moses?
Does this story have a happy ending?

Story 25: The Families-of-Israel Enter the Land of Israel

The Torah has a happy ending.
Both of God's promises finally come true.
It is also a little bit sad.

Long ago, God promised
Abraham and Sarah two things:
"Your family will grow into a great nation.
Your family will own the Land of Israel."
It took Abraham and Sarah
a very long time
to even have one child.

Isaac and Rebekkah took over.
They helped to increase the family.

Jacob, Rachel and Leah
took over.
They increased the family
even more.
It was still only a family.

Joseph took the family
away from Canaan.
They were still
only seventy people.
They were no longer
in the land that would
become Israel.
They kept on hoping.

In Egypt there was
good news and bad news.
The family grew into a nation.
They were now the Families-of-Israel.
They also became slaves.

God took them out of Egypt.
Moses led them in the desert.
They went to Mount Sinai.
They met God.

They built the *Mishkan*.
There were good times.
There were problems.
Now the Torah is ready to end.

Moses was very old.
He had lived 120 years.
Moses picked a new leader for the Jewish people.
The leader's name was Joshua.
Moses had led the Families-of-Israel for
40 years in the wilderness.
40 were the days and nights on the ark.
40 were the days and nights on Mt. Sinai.
40 were the years in the wilderness.
40 plus 40 plus 40 is 120.
Moses lived 120 years.

Moses climbed up Mt. Nebo to watch.
Joshua led the Families-of-Israel across the Jordan River.
They entered the Land of Israel.
God's promise came true.
Moses died knowing that the Families-of-Israel now had a home.

Hearing Questions:

How many years did Moses live?

Where did he die?

Who led the Families-of-Israel into the Land of Israel?

What were the two promises God made to Abraham and Sarah?

How does the story end?

Imagining Questions:

What was the best thing which happened in the wilderness?

What was the worst thing which ever happened in the wilderness?

Why did it take so long for God's promises to come true?

What new things can you learn the second time you read all these stories?

PARENT/TEACHER NOTES

These "retellings" of the Biblical text are close to the original. In each, I have embedded one or two nuances of understanding that come from a close reading of the original Hebrew text, and use those understandings to center these renditions. Here are some notes that may help you to see some of the connections between this retelling and the original text, and help you to share these stories and their interpretations with your children. JLG

1. CREATION: The first chapter of the Torah is really "A Song of Creation." It reads like a great poem with a chorus line—"There was evening. There was morning. The (fill in a number) day." This story also contains a secret. The first three days of creation prepare for the second set of three days. On day one God creates "light," and makes the "sun, moon, and stars" on day four. On day two God makes "sky" and "sea" while on day five God makes "fish" and "birds." On day three, God makes "dry land" and "plants," while on day six, it is time for "animals" and then "people." The story of creation is a story of preparation and then completion. God blesses all life, but God blesses people, the last thing created, with the responsibility to take charge of the entire creation. Being created in God's image comes with responsibility.

2. THE GARDEN IN EDEN: The Garden in Eden story is really a story about human relationships. It is a story about how people (and perhaps people and God) become closer through struggling with problems. It starts out with loneliness and winds up in a relationship that falls apart. Adam is lonely. No good

fit can be found. God takes a piece of Adam and makes him a partner who "comes from him." Still they do not fit. Here, the names are a secret. The "woman" who was created from "Adam's side," is first called Adam's woman (or wife). She is a role, not a person. Adam, who has named all the animals, gives her no name. Only after the chaos of the exile and the discovery that they would have a family, does he see her for who she is, and names her "Eve—the life giver."

3. BATTLING BROTHERS: CAIN & ABEL: The secret to the Cain and Abel story is that it doesn't end where we think it does. It doesn't fade to black after the murder. Rather, Cain starts over. He lives the rest of his life not being able to return to his family of origin, but by being able to start a new family. The punch line is "God even protects him." This story is not only about sibling rivalry and family tension, but about the possibility of renewal. Cain's second start is the big lesson (once we get over wanting to murder our brothers and sisters).

4. THE FLOOD: The Flood story is the story of a second creation. The very language of the story echoes the first story in the Torah—"God's breath blows across the waters," just as it does on the first day of creation. God gives the new first family a blessing, just as God did on the sixth day of creation. The key to the story is in the change in this blessing. Originally, God told people to "fill the earth and be in charge of everything." Now God tells people, "fill the earth" and "we will make a partnership." Rather than just leaving people in charge, God has a new way of working with people.

5. THE TOWER: The story of the Tower of Babel is a puzzle, a mystery. God never really explains what's wrong with people's actions. We've learned to assume (via the midrash and other interpretations) that either "trying to reach heaven" or "treating other people poorly" is the problem. In this version, we've used one of the themes in the story to underline it as a parable about the power of words and actions.

6. ABRAM, SARAI & FAMILY: Abram and Sarai are third creation, the third time that God restarts the process. When putting people in charge hasn't worked, and making a covenant with people hasn't worked either, God decides that a personal involvement with one family is the only way to help humankind learn how to live together. The Jewish people grow out of this special relationship. We are to be God's new prototype.

7. SARAH LAUGHS: This story has two themes. One theme is "God keeps promises (though it may take time). The other theme is "Hospitality is a major mitzvah." These two themes, God's promise and Sarah and Abraham's goodness, come together to create Isaac, their son.

8. SODOM GOES BOOM: The Sodom story is the place in the Torah where the theme of justice is rooted. Its best sound bite is Abraham yelling at God, "Will not the Judge of the cosmos do justice?" The Sodom story is paired with the story of Lot leaving. One story leads into the other. The peace of Abraham's camp breaks down—and we suspect issues of justice. There is fighting between Lot's shepherds and Abraham's herdsmen. We sort of know (without being told) that it is a fight over who owns what. They split. Lot chooses the rich, but not so moral, territory of Sodom. He gets there and finds that his family is the only good family in town. They hang onto some of their values (still offering hospitality just as Abraham does) but his goodness is still overwhelmed by the corruption of the city. His wife is lost in the turmoil.

9. REBEKKAH REALLY CARES: This is a great love story. The simple essence of this story is that Rebekkah is the perfect next mother for the Jewish people because she shares the family values. She runs and hurries to welcome strangers just the way that Abraham and Sarah do.

10. BATTLING BROTHERS: JACOB & ESAU: This story understands that Jacob and Esau are always fighting. They are those kind of brothers. Unlike Cain and Abel, no one gets killed. We sense that Esau is the athlete, Jacob the Rhodes scholar. Jacob is always tricking Esau. He does it twice (that we can see). In the end, Jacob has "stolen" the family birthright and the family blessing. When one reads the Torah, one has to ask if Isaac was really fooled by Jacob pretending to be his brother, Esau, and sneaking in to get the family blessing. The text is pretty unclear on the issue. We begin to suspect, but we will never know for sure, that Isaac knew what was happening, was not fooled by the costume, and blessed Jacob anyway.

11. JACOB'S DREAM: Jacob leaves home in a turmoil. Things have fallen apart. He is alone and unsure. Out of this moment of doubt, of loss, he meets God. God often seems to be there in our need, rather than at our intellectual desire.

12. ISRAEL'S FAMILY: The story of Leah and Rachel parallels the story of Jacob and Esau. The two struggle and "wrestle" with each other; however, they find a way to live together. Despite the tension (and probably because of it) the nation of Israel is born. In the story's other theme, Jacob remembers and keeps his promise to God.

13. THE WRESTLING MATCH: The wrestling match is the closing parenthesis on the Jacob story. It is the third fight. The first two were between Jacob and Esau. Here it is with a stranger/angel/God. Whatever happens in this strange night encounter, it closes off all the conflict and allows for a peaceful meeting between brothers the next day. What is wonderful is that as Jacob struggles, he relearns the lesson he had learned in his night flight at Bet El (the opening parenthesis). Even when we don't know it, God is in this place. Even in our inner struggles, even when things are darkest, God is there.

14. JOESPH: THE FAVORITE: Joseph is like Jacob, a younger son who is favored. Like his father he struggles with his brother(s). Like Jacob he dreams. Like Jacob, God is with him, but more distant. Joseph is the bridge between Jacob and Moses. Through him, we take Judaism on the road to Egypt, and grow from family to nation. In that process, we retell key stories (dreams, fights, resolutions, and a covenant with God) and take it a step further. The Joseph cycle fills four parashot (1/4 of Genesis). It is the Torah's big epic. In the first part, we set the stage, and have Joseph's first "fall" into the pit.

15. JOSEPH GOES TO JAIL AND THEN WORKS FOR PHARAOH: The second story, the early Egypt saga, is the heart of the Joseph story. We work with two ideas. One is the notion that everything in the Joseph story happens twice. Two falls into "pits," three sets of two dreams, two rises from the "pits," etc. This is centralized when Joseph tells Pharaoh that he had two dreams to prove that they came from God. In Jewish law, it always takes two witnesses to establish a fact. The double events in the Joseph story are the "proof" that God is going to bring Israel into Egypt (which is a pit), stay with them, and then lead them to great success. The entire book of Exodus is foreshadowed in this story. The second insight grows out of the fact that Joseph looks lucky. It sounds like a story of "great luck." But, it is not luck. It is God. Over and over, the Torah says, "But God was with Joseph." Our narrative seeks to discuss the idea that God's presence isn't luck.

16. AND FINALLY—JACOB COMES TO EGYPT: This third section of the Joseph story—Joseph gets even—is the one that is shorter than I would have liked. In the battle to "fit it all into one short enough book" some things have to go. We have, in essence, two stories here. The first is the "turn around is fair play" saga where Joseph gets the family to bow to him just like the dreams at the beginning. This is a test to see if they have changed. The second is the reunion with his father, Jacob, and the passing of the baton to a generation of tribal leaders rather than a single patriarch.

17. BABY MOSES: The Moses story starts with lots of echoes of Genesis. Moses is "good" just like creation. He is saved by an "ark" of bulrushes and pitch, just like Noah and family. He is connected to Pharaoh, just as Joseph. God's long-awaited plan kicks in. Slavery begins and, hopefully, there is a way out.

18. THE BURNING BUSH: The burning bush story takes us to Mt. Sinai. In many ways, it is a foreshadowing of the Ten Commandments story. Moses leads a flock of sheep there. God meets them in a miraculous fiery appearance. Through Moses, the Jewish people get direction. The theme of remembering and keeping promises, which started with Sarah and Abraham, has a major reprise.

19. BLOOD, FROGS, LICE, WILD ANIMALS, SICK COWS, BOILS, HAIL, LOCUSTS, DARKNESS, AND A VISIT FROM THE ANGEL OF DEATH:
The story of the ten plagues is complicated by our reaction. On the surface it is a cartoon of the bad guys getting their just desserts. Therefore, the Nile, which is where they killed Jewish babies, is turned to blood because it was already bloody. In the end, Egyptian sons die, just as Jewish sons had died. As it moves from cartoon toward an emotional reality with much suffering and death, it becomes darker. We ask, why is this fair. We then confront the idea of the hardened heart. On the surface in the Torah, God hardens Pharaoh's heart—and it therefore prevents him from changing. When you read more closely, you realize that Pharaoh actually hardened his own heart (a nuance that is not directly expressed in the kids' text—but allowed for in the language, "His heart was hard!"). We begin to understand that Pharaoh's monomania (like the Nazi's diverting trains away from the war effort to kill more Jews) leads to his destruction. We ask—when are our hearts too hardened by our obsessions?

20. MIRIAM'S SONG:
Read the Torah carefully and women are the heroes (or, if you prefer, heroines) of the Exodus. Moses is "passed" from mother to Pharaoh's daughter, to his sister Miriam, to Tziporah his wife. The midwives are the ones who saved Jewish children. In the midrash, women do even more of the saving of Jews by protecting the Jewish future by bearing children and giving them Hebrew names, etc. There is much in the conjunction between women's strength and courage and the way we got out of Egypt. In spinning the story of the Reed Sea away from Moses and toward Miriam, I've used a major event (well popularized in popular Jewish culture) to make sure that women have their day in the Torah, too.

21. THE TEN COMMANDMENTS:
The Ten Commandments moment is the heart of the Jewish experience. Its origins go back to Abram and Sarai moving to the Land of Canaan because of God's promises. It's future stretches forward to the Messiah. This is the pivotal moment. Finally, the Jewish people are face-to-face with God—and this relationship is a moment of Torah study, not ritual.

22. THE GOLDEN CALF:
There are two ways of looking at the Golden Calf story. One is to say that bad people led the Jewish people to make mistakes. The Torah (not our text) places some of the blame for the Golden Calf on the mixed multitude. The other way is to say that we all have our moments of fear where we give into idols rather than our deeper faith. We each make golden calves. The power point in the story is that God gives the people a way out. The story ends with *T'shuvah*, repentance. We, too, get to start over.

23. GOD LIVES IN THE MIDDLE OF THE FAMILIES-OF-ISRAEL:
Most people writing a children's Bible would skip the Tabernacle. We couldn't for two reasons: (1) kids think the Tabernacle is neat. (2) The idea that we can build places where God is our neighbor is too important to skip. The beauty in the Tabernacle story is the way it echoes the creation of the world. Just as God built the world so people could live, we build the Tabernacle so that God can be close to us.

24. MOSES HITS THE ROCK: The Rock story teaches that everyone makes mistakes. It is the "even Moses is human" story in the Torah. The rabbis noticed that the big fight around the rock happened right after Miriam died. They saw that the Torah was teaching that when we are sad and angry, often our actions get out of control. That is true for the people demanding water in a mean way, and it is true of Moses' losing his cool and striking out. The hard lesson of this story is that even when there are "extenuating circumstances" we are still responsible for our actions. The good news is that as hard as it is for one generation to retire, doing so always makes room for the next.

25. THE FAMILIES-OF-ISRAEL ENTER THE LAND OF ISRAEL: We use "the death of Moses" story as a way of reviewing the Torah, to realize that the process begun with the "Tree of Knowledge" connects us to Mt. Sinai. A covenant made with Abram and Sarai takes us out of Egypt. The dreams that Jacob had lead us into the Land of Israel. These stories do not stand alone, but weave into one another. In that weaving, they enter the fabric of our hearts and souls, too. The promises come true. The promises are still to be completed.